D0891751

PEOPLE OF CHARACTER

Thomas Jefferson

A Life of Patriotism

Written by Tonya Leslie
Illustrated by Tina Walski

BELLWETHER MEDIA • MINNEAPOLIS, MN

Note to Librarians, Teachers, and Parents:

Blastoff! Readers are carefully developed by literacy experts and combine standards-based content with developmentally-appropriate text.

Level 1 provides the most support through repetition of high-frequency words, light text, predictable sentence patterns, and strong visual support.

Level 2 offers early readers a bit more challenge through varied simple sentences, increased text load, and less repetition of high frequency words.

Level 3 advances early-fluent readers toward fluency through increased text and concept load, less reliance on visuals, longer sentences, and more literary language.

Level 4 builds reading stamina by providing more text per page, increased use of punctuation, greater variation in sentence patterns, and increasingly challenging vocabulary.

Level 5 encourages children to move from "learning to read" to "reading to learn" by providing even more text, varied writing styles, and less familiar topics.

Whichever book is right for your reader, Blastoff! Readers are the perfect books to build confidence and encourage a love of reading that will last a lifetime!

This edition first published in 2008 by Bellwether Media.

Library of Congress Cataloging-in-Publication Data
Leslie, Tonya.
Thomas Jefferson : a life of patriotism / by Tonya Leslie.
p. cm. – (Blastoff! readers : people of character)
Includes bibliographical references and index.
Audience: Grades 4-6.
ISBN-13: 978-1-60014-093-8 (hardcover : alk. paper)
ISBN-10: 1-60014-093-9 (hardcover : alk. paper)
1. Jefferson, Thomas, 1743 - 1826–Juvenile literature. 2. Patriotism–Juvenile literature. 3. Presidents–United States–Biography–Juvenile literature. I. Title.

E332.79.L47 2008
973.4'6092–dc22 2007025828

Contents

Is your country a great place to live? **Patriotism** is loving your country. It is also giving your time and talents to make your country a great place. Thomas Jefferson was the third President of the United States and he was a patriot. He spent much of his life helping the young United States succeed.

Thomas was born in Virginia in 1743 and came from a well-known family. As a young man, he studied to be a lawyer and worked in **government**. He was very smart and an excellent writer. He could explain important ideas about how government worked and how it might work even better. People respected him and saw him as a leader.

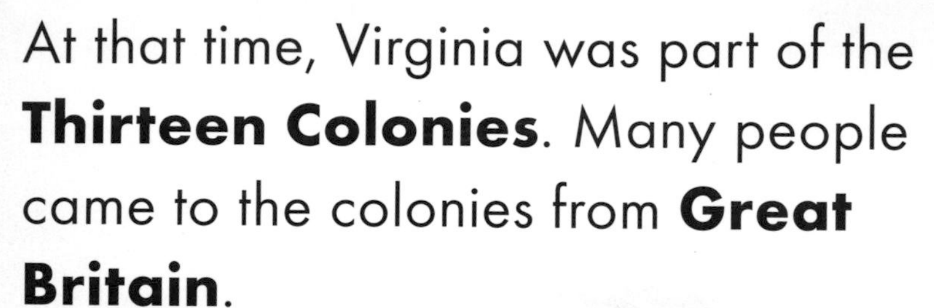

At that time, Virginia was part of the **Thirteen Colonies**. Many people came to the colonies from **Great Britain**.

They wanted the freedom to practice their own religion and the opportunity to build a better life.

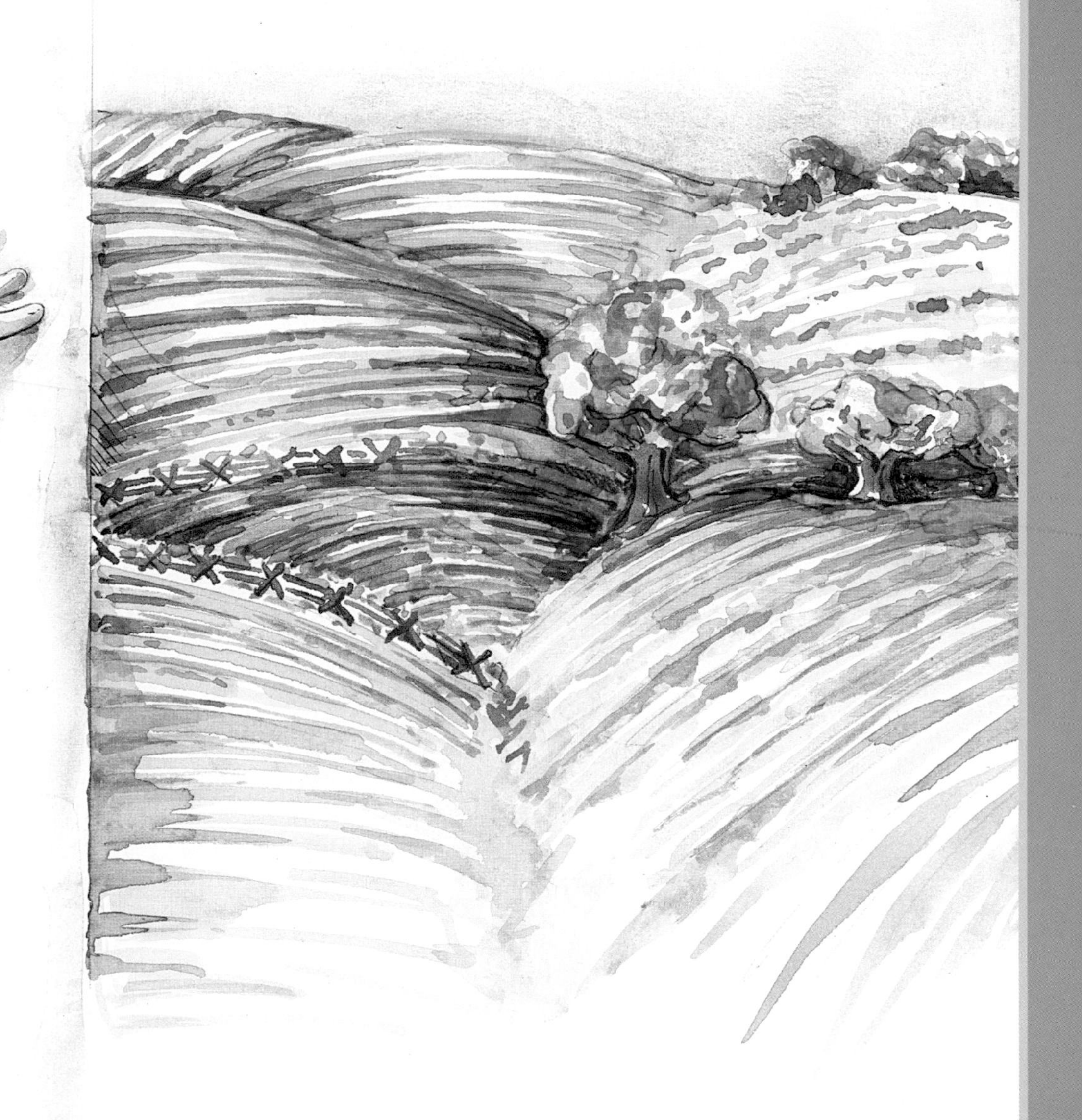

The colonies were ruled by Great Britain. The people in the colonies became angry because Great Britain made unfair laws and forced them to pay high **taxes**.

The colonists wanted to make their own laws. But Great Britain did not want to give up its power.

This conflict grew into a war between Great Britain and the colonies in 1775. It was called the **Revolutionary War**. It was a fight for the **independence** of the colonies. Many colonial leaders felt they needed more than weapons to win the war. They also needed strong words.

They needed to tell the world they were starting a new government. They needed to say their government would have its own fair laws.

The leaders asked Thomas to write these strong words in a **declaration**. Some leaders shared their thoughts and ideas with Thomas. He combined their ideas with his own and wrote a declaration. Could Thomas explain the important new ideas using pen and paper? Could Thomas write words that would start a brand new government?

He did! Thomas wrote the **Declaration of Independence**. It said the colonies would be independent from Great Britain. It also said all men had equal **rights** and the government should always protect these rights. Everyone agreed Thomas' words captured the spirit of the new America. On July 4, 1776, the leaders accepted it. Many leaders signed it to show their support.

After the Declaration of Independence was signed, it took many more years of fighting before the colonists won the war.

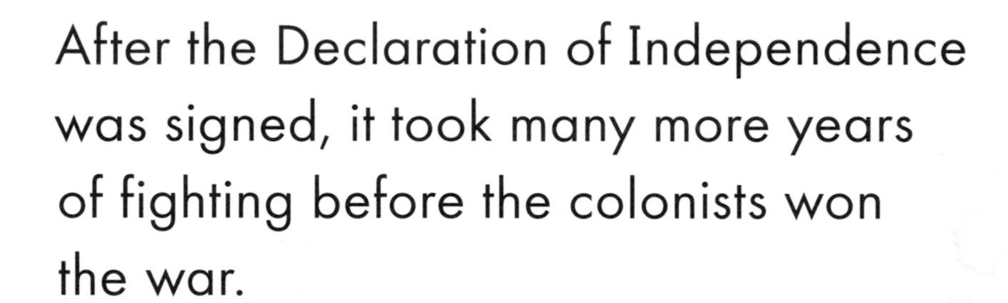

In 1783, the war was finally over. The colonists had won their independence. They could now begin forming the government of the United States of America.

After the war, Thomas continued to devote his life to the United States. He became vice president and then president. He died at the age of eighty-three, fifty years after writing the Declaration of Independence. Thomas is remembered for being one of the first and greatest American patriots. There are many famous **monuments** in his honor, but you don't have to go far to see Thomas. Look for him the next time you see a nickel.

Glossary

declaration–a written statement or announcement

Declaration of Independence–the declaration written by Thomas Jefferson in 1776 that announced the independence of the American colonies from Great Britain

government–a system of control and direction for a group of people

Great Britain–an island in Europe made up of England, Scotland, and Wales

independence–the state of being free from the control of another person or government

monument–a structure built to honor a person or event

patriotism–love and support for one's country

Revolutionary War–the war for American independence from Great Britain (1775-1783)

right–something a person deserves to have

taxes–money taken to support the government

Thirteen Colonies–the thirteen British colonies in North America that joined together to become the United States of America

To Learn More

AT THE LIBRARY

Barrett, Marvin. *Meet Thomas Jefferson*. New York: Random House, 1989.

Bobrick, Benson. *Fight for Freedom: The Revolutionary War*. New York: Atheneum, 2004.

Davis, Kenneth. *Don't Know Much About Thomas Jefferson*. New York: Harper Trophy, 2005.

ON THE WEB

Learning more about Thomas Jefferson is as easy as 1, 2, 3.

1. Go to www.factsurfer.com
2. Enter "Thomas Jefferson" into search box.
3. Click the "Surf" button and you will see a list of related web sites.

With factsurfer.com, finding more information is just a click away.

Index